TREASURES OF
THE SPANISH MAIN

TREASURES OF THE SPANISH MAIN

by

Dorothy Hinshaw Patent

BENCHMARK BOOKS

MARSHALL CAVENDISH
NEW YORK

Acknowledgments

*With gratitude to Dr. Eugene Lyon,
historian, for his helpful reading of the text.*

*With thanks, too, to Duncan Mathewson and
Cory Malcolm for their help.*

Benchmark Books
Marshall Cavendish Corporation
99 White Plains Road
Tarrytown, New York 10591-9001

Library of Congress Cataloging-in-Publication Data
Patent, Dorothy Hinshaw.
Treasures of the Spanish Main / Dorothy Hinshaw Patent.
p.   cm. — (Frozen in time)
Includes bibliographical references and index.
Summary: Presents background information about the sinking of the Spanish galleon,
Atocha, in 1622 and describes efforts to locate the wreck and successfully salvage its
treasure more than 300 years later.
ISBN 0-7614-0786-3
1. Nuestra Señora de Atocha (Ship)—Juvenile literature. 2. Treasure-trove—Florida—
Juvenile literature. [1. Nuestra Señora de Atocha (Ship). 2. Buried treasure.]
I. Title. II. Series:
Patent, Dorothy Hinshaw. Frozen in time.
G530.N83P38   1999   975.9'41—dc21   99—32141   CIP   AC

Printed in Hong Kong

1 3 5 6 4 2

Photo research by Linda Sykes Picture Research, Hilton Head, SC
Book design by Carol Matsuyama

Photo Credits
Front cover: Courtesy of Bridgeman Art Library International, Ltd.; title pages 2–3,
10–11, 22, 43; Wendy Tucker, page 7; Mel Fisher Maritime Center, Key West, Florida:
Dylan Kibler, pages 8, 34, 54; Scott Nierling, pages 9, 31, 38, 40, 47, 50 (top & bottom),
53; Don Kincaid, pages 24–25, 30; Pat Clyne, pages 27, 28, 35, 36, 45; Richard
Schlect/National Geographic Society Image Collection: page 15; Rijksmuseum,
Amsterdam: pages 16–17; New York Public Library: pages 18–19; North Wind Pictures:
page 20; Art Resource: page 23; Christie's Images: pages 41, 51; Bob Mack: page 42;
Hispanic Society, NY: page 49.

Contents

Introduction

Treasure!

Treasure! The word makes our hearts beat fast. We think of chests full of silver and gold coins, fabulous jewelry, heavy gold and silver bars. Such treasure does lie on the bottom of the sea, waiting to be found. And every once in a while, determined treasure hunters strike it rich.

How did great wealth end up in the ocean? From the time of Christopher Columbus until the nineteenth century, the Spanish ruled Florida, Mexico, many islands of the Caribbean Sea, and much of Central and South America. The seas they controlled in the New World came to be called the Spanish Main. For many years, the Spanish mined

Mel Fisher holds up a few gold treasures from the Ghost Galleons as he kneels behind a bronze cannon from the Atocha.

quantities of silver, gold, and precious gems from their American colonies. They sent the valuable cargo by fleets of ships to the mother country across the Atlantic Ocean.

Getting the priceless treasure all the way from the Americas to Spain wasn't easy. The ships had to pass by the Florida Keys, a group of islands that lie between the Gulf of Mexico and the Caribbean Sea. These islands, with their rocky reefs and shallow waters, were dangerous, especially during hurricane season. Dozens of Spanish ships met their end among the Florida Keys.

One of these, the Nuestra Señora de Atocha (new-ES-tra seen-YOUR-a day ah-TOE-cha) was a galleon—a certain kind of ship—with an especially valuable cargo. When it sank in 1622, the Atocha was carrying a treasure of silver and gold worth hundreds of millions of dollars. The Spanish tried to salvage this cargo but failed. More than three hundred years later, treasure hunters with modern equipment still could not find the ship. By the end of the 1960s, the Atocha and its sister ship, the Santa Margarita, had been nicknamed the Ghost Galleons of 1622 because they had eluded treasure hunters for so long.

In 1969 a man named Mel Fisher became determined to find the Ghost Galleons. He and his crew searched relentlessly. They found some items such as gold jewelry and a few silver bars. But it took sixteen years of hunting before they finally hit the jackpot by locating the main cargo of the Atocha. This "mother lode" and other finds from both ships contained not just precious treasure. They also held many items that help us understand today what life was like more than 375 years ago.

When I heard about the Atocha, I decided to see the items from the Ghost Galleons for myself. Some of them are on display at the Mel Fisher Maritime Heritage Society, a museum in Key West, one of the islands in the Florida Keys. As I drove toward the museum, I could see why the Keys were so treacherous for the Spanish ships. Dozens of these tiny green islands lie scattered in an arc stretching from the tip of the Florida mainland out into the ocean. In between the islands, coral reefs lurk underneath the shallow waters. The Spanish ships, powered by sails, were helpless before the hurricane winds that forced them against the reefs and islands.

In the museum, I admired the delicate workmanship of a magnificent gold and emerald cross found lying in a silver box, along with a dazzling emerald ring. In the display cases, gold chains gleamed like new, even after hundreds of years underwater. More ordinary objects reminded me of how different life was in those times. The silver top for a brazier, a pan that held glowing coals to warm a passenger's cabin, told of an age before electricity. The abundant cannonballs and smaller shot spoke of the hazards caused by pirates.

Every item recovered from the Ghost Galleons had its own story to tell about life in those times, and I was eager to learn as much as I could about those stories.

1

THE FATE OF THE GHOST GALLEONS

Early on the morning of Sunday, September 4, 1622, a Spanish treasure fleet set sail from Havana, Cuba, for Spain. The winds were mild and favorable. There were twenty-eight ships in the fleet, including the *Atocha* and the *Santa Margarita*. They carried gold, silver, emeralds, jewelry, and other valuable cargo gathered in the New World. The fabulous treasure was vital to the Spanish king, who needed it urgently. It would help him pay for expensive wars

◄ *A Spanish galleon like this one could carry cargo as well as help defend a fleet of ships.*

and royal luxuries. Time was of the essence. Already it was six weeks into the hurricane season. In spite of the risks, the treasure fleet set out.

The ships' route would take them eastward, then north toward the Florida Keys to enter the Gulf Stream. This northbound current would carry them quickly up the Florida coast. Beyond there, the Spaniards expected to catch the trade winds blowing eastward toward home.

They would never get that far.

The Storm

After leaving Havana, the ships made good time at first. Toward dawn on Monday, they entered the Gulf Stream. A strong northeast wind was blowing against the current, creating big waves that made progress difficult. Crews prepared to deal with the storm by taking down some of the sails and securing loose objects on deck. Soon the mariners were experiencing a full-blown hurricane. The wind screamed and the waves grew huge. Controlling the *Atocha*, which was overloaded, became almost impossible. Water tumbled over the middle section of the deck as the ship pitched and swayed.

All the ships had to struggle to stay afloat. The masts of some were ripped away by the wind. Many lost their rudders. As darkness fell once more, the ships and their passengers found themselves at the mercy of the sea.

During the night, the wind shifted and began to blow from the south. Fortunately, most of the ships had already made it past the dangerous shallow waters and coral reefs at the southern end of the Florida Keys. The *Atocha*, the *Santa Margarita*, and three other vessels, however, had not managed to get so far.

The crews of these ships tried to prevent their vessels from going aground by dropping anchor. But their efforts failed, because the anchors would not hold. There was a saying of the times, "as meager as a Spanish anchor," meaning the anchors were poorly designed. Although they weighed about a ton each, their shafts were too long and thin to bear the weight of a heavily loaded ship. They often bent or broke completely. The Spanish ships were helpless against the south wind, which threatened to blow them right up into the shallows and destroy them.

Destroy them it did. The *Santa Margarita* ended up being blown across a reef and grounded on a sandbar, shattered by the storm. A huge wave lifted the *Atocha* and dropped it onto a reef, where its hull was ripped open. The waves then carried the wounded ship forward into the water, where it sank, weighted down by ballast and treasure.

When the storm finally passed, the crewmen of the merchant ship *Santa Cruz* did what they could to find survivors. They managed to rescue sixty-eight people from the *Margarita*. But when they came upon the remains of the *Atocha*, they found only five people clinging to bits of wreckage: one sailor, two apprentice sailors, and two black slaves. One hundred and forty-three people on the *Margarita* and two hundred and sixty on the *Atocha* had drowned.

The Passenger List

On the *Atocha*'s fatal voyage, forty-eight private passengers were on board. They included noblemen and noblewomen, merchants, a surgeon, and an important church official. All their names were listed on the passenger register. In addition, eight servants and slaves traveled on the ship. Their names weren't listed, for they were thought of as "persons of no importance."

The Treasure Fleets

Christopher Columbus's voyages of discovery in the late 1400s and early 1500s opened up the New World for Spain. The Renaissance period was under way in Europe, with science, art, trade, and business all beginning to flourish. Money was power, providing the means to build up armies and buy goods and property. Today we use paper to represent wealth. A paper bill that says one hundred dollars on it can be used to buy one hundred dollars' worth of goods. But in those days, money meant metals: copper, gold, and silver. Coins were made from the amount of metal they were actually worth. So Spain's conquest of the Americas, with their abundance of precious metals, greatly increased the nation's power.

By the early 1600s, Spain controlled a world empire. It held lands not only in Europe and the Americas, but also in Africa and Asia. The Philippines was an important colony. Spain grew rich and powerful as it acquired goods from around the world. Spanish ships, calling at ports in Asia and America, picked up precious metals, gems, agricultural products, and other valuables. These riches, however, were worthless unless they could be safely carried over the vast Atlantic Ocean to Spain.

The Spanish organized their ships into fleets. The fleets that carried much of the gold, silver, and other precious cargo were known as the treasure fleets. A kind of ship called the galleon usually carried the most valuable cargo. Galleons were well armed, and their guns protected the other ships in the fleet as well as their own cargo.

The system of fleets was quite complicated. The Manila Fleet, which took on its cargo in the Philippines, carried silk, expensive dyes, porcelain, gems, and spices from Asia to Acapulco on the western coast of New Spain (now Mexico). There the goods were loaded on mules and taken overland to Veracruz on the Gulf of Mexico.

Meanwhile, the South Seas Fleet loaded up in the town of Callao, on the coast of Peru. It carried silver, emeralds, and other valuables from Peruvian and Chilean mines. The ships stopped at Guayaquil, in Ecuador, to pick up more treasure. They then landed in Panama, where they unloaded their cargo. Mules transported it overland to Portobelo on the Caribbean side.

While the cargo from the colonies was being gathered, ships were also coming to the New World from Spain. They made up the Tierra Firme Fleet. This fleet carried wine, cloth, olive oil, mercury (used in mining silver), and other supplies from Spain to the New World. As the ships dropped off their cargo in various ports, they were loaded with the valuables from the colonies. The *Atocha* and *Santa Margarita* were part of the Tierra Firme Fleet. At the same time, two other fleets of ships—known as the New Spain and the Honduras Fleets—also picked up cargo bound for Spain.

The sailing of the fleets was planned so

The map shows the routes of the Spanish treasure fleet. Below, an artist imagines the breakup of the Santa Margarita during the hurricane of 1622.

that they would all meet in Havana, Cuba, by early summer. From there, they would make the Atlantic crossing together. In this way, treasure and trade goods from Asia and America made their way to the mother country. Small private ships joined the fleets in order to sail under the protection of the armed galleons. Private citizens with their own goods also traveled on the galleons.

On that fateful journey in 1622, the *Atocha* and the *Santa Margarita* carried much of the Spanish treasure. The *Atocha* was assigned the job of *almiranta*, protecting the slow merchant ships from the rear.

2

LOST TREASURE

The Spanish were shocked to learn of the fate of the fleet. Besides the *Atocha* and the *Santa Margarita*, another galleon, the *Rosario*, had been wrecked, as well as two smaller ships. Altogether, 550 people had been lost, along with valuable cargo and the treasure desperately needed by the Spanish king.

Attempts at Retrieval

An experienced seaman, Gaspar de Vargas, began recovery efforts. One of the *Atocha*'s masts was visible above the water, but divers found that the ship's hatches were sealed. The wreck was resting at fifty-five feet (16.8 meters), the limit for a diver's lungs. After retrieving two cannons from the deck, the crew

Dutch ships attack a Spanish treasure fleet in this old woodcut. English and Dutch ships as well as pirates were common threats to the Spanish at sea. ➤

Even hundreds of years ago, people had a variety of methods for recovering lost treasure. Here, salvagers work to recover treasure from a sunken ship in 1788. Note the diver on the right and the diving bell in the center.

looked in vain for the *Santa Margarita*, then located the *Rosario*. Fortunately, that galleon lay in the shallows, so Vargas's workers were able to recover the full treasure.

On October 5, 1622, as the salvage of the *Rosario* was nearly completed, another hurricane struck. This storm was even worse than the first. Enormous waves furiously battered the wreck of the *Atocha*. The bow section was broken off in one piece, and the sterncastle and gun deck were ripped off together. The storm carried both parts away, scattering bits and pieces of wreckage along their paths. But the lower hull of the ship, weighted down by ballast, copper bars, and the bulk of the silver treasure, remained on the floor of the sea.

Without the mast peeking above the water to mark the site, Vargas and his men had trouble locating the wreck. The divers could barely reach bottom without getting out of breath, and winter weather made the salvage attempt dangerous. Finally, Vargas called off his crew and wrote a report requesting trained pearl divers from the Caribbean. They were his only hope for retrieving the treasure.

In late February 1623, salvage efforts were renewed. But even as the new divers worked, sand accumulated over the wreck, and only a small amount of silver was recovered. The attempt had been a failure.

Finding the *Santa Margarita*

In June 1626, salvager Francisco Melián (mel-ee-AHN) had better luck. He had a diving bell made to locate the lost galleons. A diving bell was a device that allowed people to breathe underwater. It was a fairly large, bell-shaped structure in which people could sit. It was open to the water at the bottom. A hose supplied air from the surface. The air pressure within the bell kept the water out of the device.

Using the diving bell, one of Melián's slave workers

The Spanish Galleon

T he galleon (GAL-ee-un) was developed during the sixteenth century, when ships sailing the vast Pacific and Atlantic Oceans needed to be able to fight as well as to sail. Before that time, the main type of fighting vessel was the galley. It was powered by the oars of slaves and prisoners. Galleys were popular ships in the Mediterranean Sea. But galleys weren't practical for ocean voyages—too much food would have to be stored on board to feed the oarsmen. So shipbuilders combined the qualities of two kinds of vessels—the caravel and the carrack—to create the galleon. From the caravel, a small, light sailing ship, came the ability to change direction quickly. The design of the carrack provided the large cargo area needed for long ocean voyages. Columbus's ship the *Santa Maria* was a carrack.

All the major European countries used galleons during the late sixteenth and the seventeenth centuries. A galleon was easy to recognize. It featured a high rear section called the sterncastle, which rose as much as thirty-five feet (10.7 meters) above the waterline. A slightly raised forecastle stood at the front, or bow, end of the ship. A galleon was shaped like a fish, with a rounded bow and a slim stern. Its length was three or four times its middle width. It took about two thousand sturdy oak trees to build one galleon. The *Atocha*, a typical galleon, was one hundred feet (thirty meters) long and weighed five hundred and fifty tons. It had three masts, each of which carried two or three sails. Other sails were hoisted, or raised, up front on a long pole called the bowsprit.

At the very bottom of the ship, large river stones were loaded as ballast—weight to help give the ship stability. Most of the cargo was stored above the ballast. The next deck up, called the orlop, was at or below the waterline. Cannonballs, sails, and anchor cables were all stored on the orlop deck. Some of the crew had to sleep there, too. Next came the gun deck. Here cannon barrels stuck out from holes in the sides of the ship. These were the main defense of the galleon. Many of the crew members slept here, with the officers' quarters toward the stern. The top deck was open to the air in the middle of the ship. Toward the front, the protected forecastle provided quarters for some of the sailors. The sterncastle held cabins for wealthy passengers and for the captain.

When a galleon was built, the lower sides and bottom were constructed first. Everything from the gun deck up was attached to this frame, or hull. Being built in sections like this meant that galleons often broke into a number of pieces when they became shipwrecked, as did the *Atocha*.

found the wreck of the *Margarita*. As a reward, the slave was given his freedom. Over the summer, Melián's workers recovered a large portion of the *Margarita*'s treasure.

For the next twenty years, Melián continued to search for the *Atocha*. His final effort, in 1643, failed, and he died in 1644. By that time, the Spanish empire had begun to fade. A few more attempts were made to locate the missing *Atocha*. But by 1676, hope was given up. For more than three hundred years, the remains of the Ghost Galleon rested peacefully on the floor of the sea.

Spain in the Age of Exploration

Spain was the greatest power in the Western world during the sixteenth and seventeenth centuries, a time known as the Age of Exploration. This exciting period began with the help of Ferdinand and Isabella, the Spanish monarchs who funded Columbus's voyage to America in 1492. Not long after, Spain set out to conquer the New World. Soon it controlled Mexico and most of Central and South America, the region we now call Latin America.

In addition to conquering much of the New World, Spain gained control of the Philippines in the early 1500s and discovered a belt of wind that blew westward from there toward the coast of South America. Spain tied its empire together by shipping Asian goods out of the Philippines to the New World and combining that cargo with the treasures from the New World.

During this period of Spain's power, the country was ruled by a series of kings descended from Ferdinand and Isabella. Philip II ruled from 1556 to 1598. He was a strong king whose mission in life was to spread the power of Spain and the Catholic Church around the world. During his reign, Spain took over the Portuguese empire, including Brazil. He also made war with England. England had established a Protestant church, and the Spanish wanted badly to restore the Roman Catholic Church there. In addition, the English had been raiding Spanish ports and ships, especially along the eastern coast of South America, interfering with the flow of treasure from the New World to Spain. In 1588 the king sent the warships of the Spanish Armada to invade England, but the great fleet was defeated.

Philip III took over from his father, Philip II, in 1598. By this time, the Spanish were having trouble managing their gigantic empire. They were constantly involved in

The incredible wealth of the Spanish royal family can be seen in the jewelry worn by Elizabeth of Valois, wife of King Philip II, in this portrait by Alonso Sanchez Coello. Similar jewelry was found on the Ghost Galleons.

Gold from the New World gloriously decorated the outfit of Philip IV and his horse in this 1635 portrait by Diego Rodríguez Valázquez.

wars in Europe, which cost a great deal of money. The lifestyle of the Spanish nobility was extravagant, and the nobility controlled government at all levels. The king and nobility relied heavily on the riches from the New World to finance their expensive tastes and military ventures. When treasure-laden ships were lost to storms, pirates, or enemy ships, the Spanish government fell further behind on paying off its creditors.

Philip IV became king in 1621, at the age of sixteen. While the Spanish empire was still the greatest in the world, it was in serious trouble. Spain was at war with

Germany. In addition, a truce that had ended conflicts with the Netherlands was broken, and war broke out between the two nations again. These military ventures, on top of the lavish spending habits of the Spanish nobility, put the country increasingly into debt. Creditors began to wait for treasure ships to sail into port. Then they would claim first rights to the silver. Most of the New World treasure went right into their hands, with little left over even to run the government. Many historians believe that the loss of the *Atocha* played a big role in the decline of Spanish world power.

3

HUNTING TREASURE

It wasn't until the 1950s that treasure hunting off the Florida coast really sprang into life. Jacques-Yves Cousteau had created a revolutionary invention—scuba, which stands for Self-Contained Underwater Breathing Apparatus. Before scuba, underwater adventures beyond the limits of human lungs depended on heavy diving suits with metal helmets. The diver got air from a long tube connected to a boat on the surface. Diving was expensive and dangerous. It was not practical when the location of a wreck wasn't known for sure. But scuba provided even the weekend

◄ *Ships from Mel Fisher's company continue to search for the remaining pieces of the* Atocha. *Mel Fisher died in late 1998.*

diver with a relatively inexpensive way to explore underwater easily. An oxygen tank, a face mask, and a pair of fins to make swimming more powerful were all that was needed.

The dreams of treasure hunters were fueled by finds such as one made by Edward Tucker off the coast of Bermuda. Tucker found a sixteenth-century Spanish ship that carried coins, silver bars, jewelry, and other items from long ago. This was the first major treasure to be salvaged in modern times, and it inspired others to try their luck.

Mel Fisher on the Scene

Many people tried to find Spanish treasure, but Mel Fisher and his company, Treasure Salvors, were the ones who finally discovered the most sought-after prize of all, the *Atocha*. While luck plays a part in such discoveries, Fisher had more than luck on his side. His greatest advantage was his personality—adventuresome, optimistic, stubborn, and willing to try new things. In addition, Fisher used every aid he could to help locate treasure and to salvage it.

Scuba wasn't the only new tool that helped the treasure hunters. Devices called magnetometers could scan the ocean floor and locate deposits of iron, which can indicate the presence of wrecks. Working with Fisher was a brilliant electronics expert named Fay Feild. He constantly fine-tuned his magnetometers, making them more and more efficient for treasure hunting.

Murky water and sand were big problems. A magnetometer might register iron, but the water was often too cloudy to see through. Fisher puzzled over the problem. He asked Feild if clear water from the surface might be directed downward by a ship's propellers. Feild designed a device that came to be called a mailbox because of its boxy shape. The mailbox was fastened to the back of the treasure hunter's boat.

The first trial of the mailbox, on a wreck in fifty feet (15.2 meters) of water, was a complete success. As Fisher described it: "It was inky

Treasure seekers often locate wrecks by using metal detectors. ➤

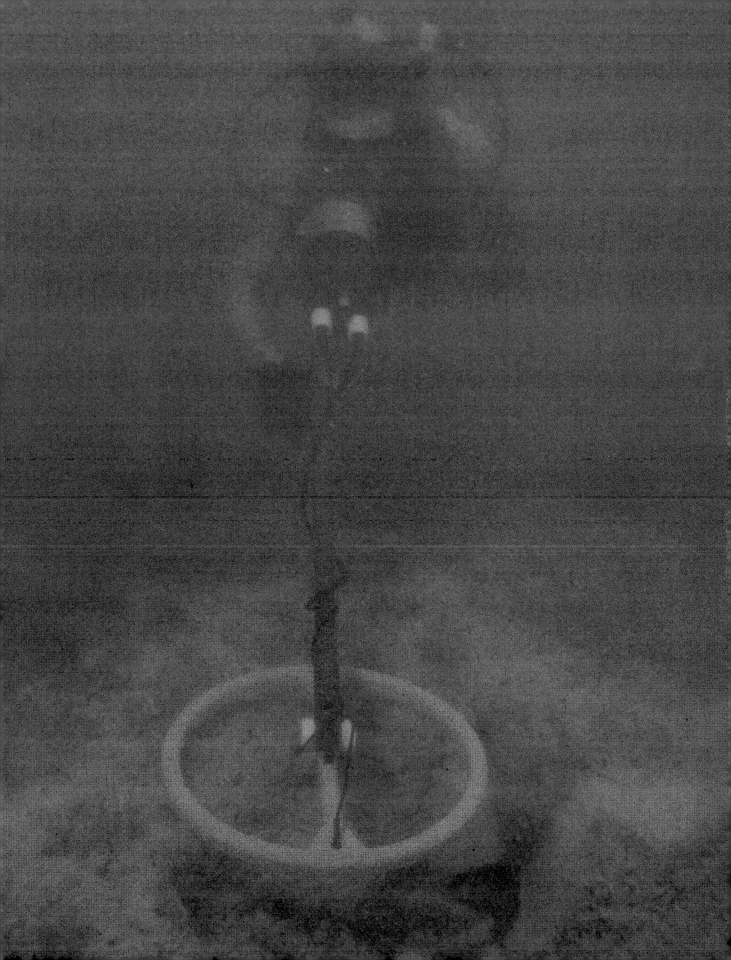

black and you couldn't see your finger in front of your mask. We turned the mailbox on slow and watched as it pushed a column of clear water right down to the bottom. We drifted down that column to the wreck, and the mailbox had made a huge bubble of clear water all around it; we could see the whole thing."

The mailbox provided a bonus as well. The force of the water dug a crater in the sand on the bottom, clearing the sand away from the wreck. From then on, mailboxes were a key to the success of Fisher's work.

Seeking the Ghost Galleons

Despite the efforts of a number of treasure hunters through 1969, including Fisher, no trace of the Ghost Galleons was found. Everyone thought the wrecks must be near the Matecumbe (mat-eh-KUM-bay) Keys in the Florida Keys—that's what Spanish documents from the time seemed to indicate. Mel Fisher, however, had faith in his magnetometers and was sure that if the wrecks were there, he would have found them.

Then Fisher learned that his friend Eugene Lyon, a historian, was going to Seville, Spain, to study old Spanish documents from the 1600s. Fisher asked Lyon to keep an eye out for any papers dealing with shipwrecks that might provide new clues about where the ships went down.

Lyon's research took place in the Archive of the Indies, which contains 40,000 bundles of documents—50 million pages in all. These documents are filled with information about the four hundred years of Spain's colonial rule in the New World. Using the archive is very difficult. The documents in a particular bundle may be about unrelated topics. In addition, they are written in a variety of hard-to-read writing. The written language is almost identical to today's Spanish. But much of the script is a peculiar form of joined, loopy letters, with no breaks

◄ *The list of cargo carried on the* Atocha *is written in an old form of Spanish, with all the words connected.*

between words or sentences. Other texts feature handwritten scrawl or letters written in a heavy, angular style known as Gothic. Time had taken its toll, too, with fire damage, wormholes, and faded ink adding to a reader's difficulties.

Dr. Eugene Lyon at work translating documents from the Atocha.

Lyon became an expert at reading the documents. While carrying out his own research, he found lists of the cargoes carried on the *Santa Margarita* and the *Atocha*. Then, glancing through another document, he happened to find a reference to the salvaging of the *Margarita* by Francisco Melián. He immediately ordered the bundle that contained the salvage documents. He hurried through them, looking for information on the location of the wreck. He came to the site people had found before—Keys of Matecumbe. But that wasn't all. The document also mentioned the Cayos del Marquéz—Keys of the Marquis. What could this mean? How could the wreck be in two places?

Lyon solved the puzzle by checking a seventeenth-century map of Florida. On that map, made after the Spanish salvage efforts, a group of islands was labeled Marquéz (mar-KAZ). These islands lay west of Key West, far from the Matecumbe Keys. A later map actually used the same phrase Lyon had found in the salvage document, Cayos del Marquéz. He had solved the mystery of why the treasure hunters hadn't found the wrecks. They had been looking more than one hundred miles (160 kilometers) from the actual site!

It turns out that at the time of the disaster all the Florida Keys were called *Matecumbe*. So when the ships sank, that word was used in documents. But later on, after the salvage efforts began, one group of islands was renamed. They were called the Marquesas (mar-KAY-

The Quinto

T he Spanish king laid claim to one-fifth of the value of all precious metals sent to Spain from the New World. This share was collected as a tax called the *quinto* (KEYN-toe). As ships headed for Spain were being loaded, each merchant had to submit his gold and silver to an official known as the silver master. The silver master prepared a document listing each gold and silver bar. The bars had already been weighed and sampled for purity. Each bar that was sent to Spain legally had many stamps on it—one for its weight, another for its purity, a third showing who owned it, and a fourth giving it a serial number. Finally, the silver master added the stamp of the royal seal, to show that the *quinto* had been paid.

Because the Spanish were such good record keepers, the members of Mel Fisher's team were able to prove that they had indeed found the wreck of the *Atocha*. They were able to match up the markings on the bars in the cargo with the list made long ago by the silver master. They also discovered that many silver and gold bars had been smuggled aboard. These bars lacked the royal seal, which meant that the *quinto* had not been paid on them.

After they have been cleaned, silver bars from the Atocha *clearly show their markings.*

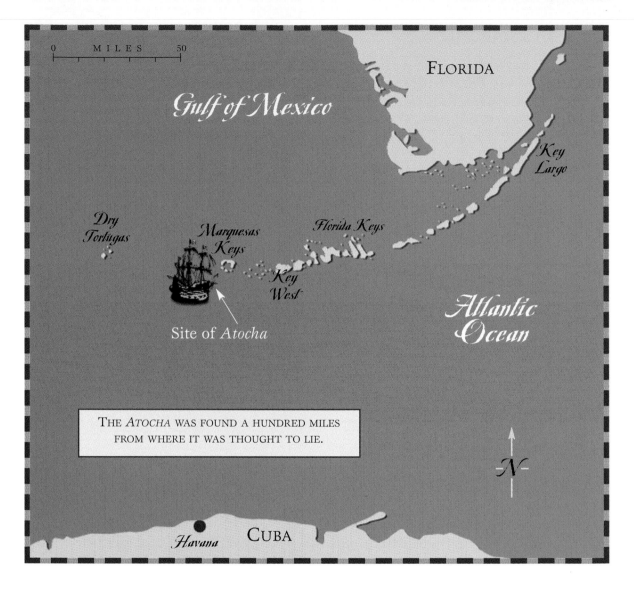

THE *ATOCHA* WAS FOUND A HUNDRED MILES FROM WHERE IT WAS THOUGHT TO LIE.

sahs) Keys, after the commanding officer of the entire convoy of fleets, the Marquis of Cadereita. Over time, other islands were also renamed, so that today only two still bear the name Matecumbe.

Finding the Ghost Galleons

As soon as Eugene Lyon told Mel Fisher of his discovery, Fisher moved his headquarters to Key West and began looking around the Marquesas Keys. At first, he searched on the wrong side of the islands. But once he was on the right track, exciting things began to happen.

On June 12, 1971, the crew found a galleon anchor. A few days later, a diver found an eight-foot-long (2.4 meters) gold chain nearby.

Despite this hopeful beginning, the search for the *Atocha* took many more years, years that sometimes brought treasure, sometimes tragedy. The son of a *National Geographic* photographer who was recording the search died accidentally in 1973. And Fisher's own son, Dirk; Dirk's wife, Angel; and diver Rick Gage drowned when their boat sank during the night on July 20, 1975. Ten years later to the day, the mother lode of the *Atocha* was finally found.

Spanish Coins in 1622

The *Atocha* and *Santa Margarita* provided a priceless window into the past largely because of the huge number of coins found in the wrecks—more than 180,000. Most of the coins were silver. They were found stuck together, covered with a crusty coating. The clumps of coins retained the shape of the plain wooden boxes in which they had been stored, quite different from the treasure chests we know from comic books and fanciful stories.

In 1622, much of the silver mined in the Americas went to Spain in the form of silver bars. But mints had been established in Mexico, Peru, Bolivia, and Colombia. A mint in Santa Fé de Bogotá, in present-day Colombia, opened in 1622. Until Mel Fisher and his crew found the galleons, coins from that mint were completely unknown.

Fewer than two hundred gold coins have been found from the two wrecks combined, because New World mints weren't allowed to make gold coins until 1621. Two of the gold coins came from the mint at Santa Fé de Bogotá. They were among the first gold coins minted in the Americas. The rest of the gold coins in the wrecks were minted in Spain and brought to the Americas.

Some of the thousands of coins the salvagers found were newly minted, but others were several years old. Interestingly, there were coins from Mexico. Since the *Atocha* and the *Margarita* carried goods from South and Central America, the presence of these coins shows that a fair amount of trade occurred among different parts of the Spanish empire.

The coinage system used at the time was based on the real (ray-AHL). One real was equal to one-eighth of an ounce of silver. The largest coin was worth eight reales (ray-AHL-es), or an ounce of silver. Smaller coins were worth from one to four reales. The term

Coins from the Atocha *fill a treasure chest. The chest shown here is a reproduction of the kind the Spanish used.*

Here is a sampling of the gold, silver, and emeralds found on the Ghost Galleons.

pieces of eight, used in pirate stories to describe coins, comes from the Spanish name for the eight-real coin.

No two coins from the find are exactly alike. That's because of the way they were made. The silver was fashioned into a long, thin bar. Then small pieces, called cobs, were cut from the bar. Each piece was placed onto a die that held the imprint for one side of the coin. Another die with the design for the other side of the coin was placed on top. Then the die was struck with a hammer, imprinting the design onto both sides of the metal. After being struck, the coin was carefully weighed, and any excess silver was trimmed off the edges.

One side of each coin was stamped with a cross, symbolizing the union of church and government that was so important in Spain. The symbol was also meant to proclaim Spain as the most powerful Catholic country in the world. In the corners of the cross stood the lions of León and the castles of Castile. The joining of these two kingdoms had united Spain and led to its domination in the world.

The other side of each coin bore the design of the Great Shield of the House of Hapsburg, the ruling family of Spain. It represents all the coats of arms of regions that Spain controlled when the Hapsburgs took over the country and its empire.

Spanish coins were the chief form of currency in much of Europe, Asia, and the Americas from the early 1500s to the early 1800s. Pieces of eight were legal tender in the United States until 1857. When an eight-real coin was cut into four pieces, each was worth two reales. The phrase *two bits*, meaning a quarter of a dollar, derives from this custom.

4

DISCOVERY

It had become a joke. For sixteen years, Mel Fisher had encouraged his crews with the words, "Today's the day." Finally, on July 20, 1985, the crackling radio voice of Mel's son Kane Fisher spoke the words everyone had been waiting to hear. "Put away the charts—we found it!" "It" was the mother lode of the *Atocha*, the main hull of the ship, laden with nearly one thousand silver bars and many other treasures. Kane and

◄ *Divers check out gold bars and other treasure on the deck of a salvage boat.*

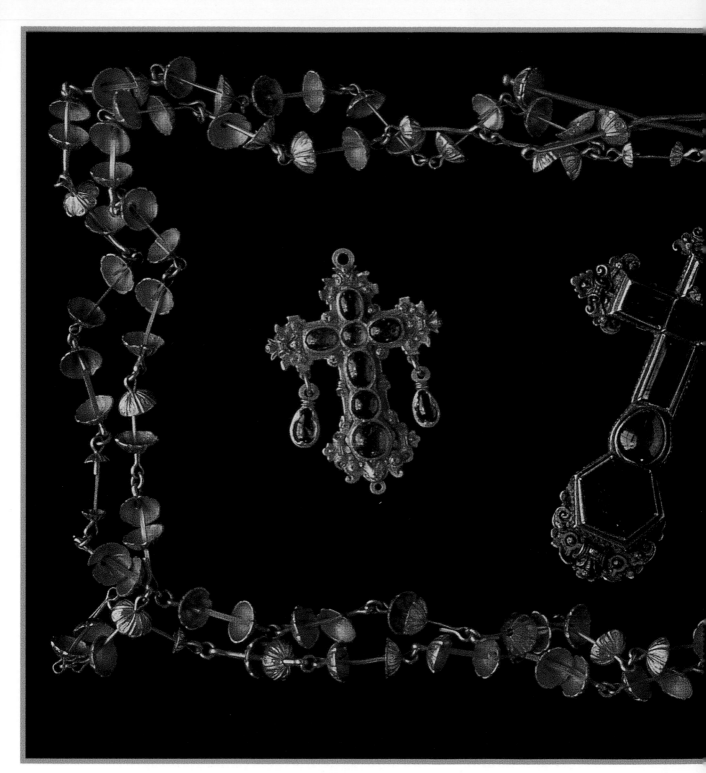

Gold and emerald jewelry from the Ghost Galleons

his divers had finally located the wreck. It lay in some fifty-five feet (16.8 meters) of water in Hawk Channel, just southwest of the Marquesas Keys. During the sixteen-year hunt, Mel Fisher's team had found precious items from both the *Atocha* and the *Santa Margarita*, including bronze guns, huge anchors weighing up to a ton each, and spectacular gold jewelry. It had been enough to keep them from giving up on the mother lode. But in the process, they had run through not only sixteen years of their lives but also eight million dollars in funds from Fisher and hundreds of other investors. Finally, the investment had paid off.

Most of the treasure was gathered during the following months. But Fisher's divers continue to this day to visit the wreck, finding emeralds and other valuables. In 1997, the crew was still bringing up rough emeralds every day, along with coins and jewelry. One emerald ring was valued at $680,000; another at $114,000. The accounting of the major treasure is impressive: so far, twenty-seven tons of silver including nearly one thousand silver bars weighing seventy pounds each and around thirty boxes of silver coins; five thousand emeralds; a chest laden with gold bars; fifteen tons of copper bars; and numerous gold chains and other beautiful jewelry.

Gold chain and coins, along with beautiful gold and emerald jewelry

Along with the treasures came many other items (called artifacts by archaeologists) that speak of life in the Spanish world more than 375 years ago. Cannons and ammunition can help archaeologists understand the details of how warfare was conducted. Pottery and other items created by native peoples in the colonies tell something about their communities. And the personal property of the passengers can bring to life the people of a different century.

Several navigating devices such as this brass astrolabe were found on the Atocha. *An astrolabe made determining the ship's latitude possible, a key to navigating at sea.*

Warfare at Sea

The treasure fleets always had to be watchful for enemies eager to steal their valuable cargo. The foes were many. Both the Dutch and the English governments were enemies of Spain. If their ships could capture Spanish treasure, they accomplished two goals. Not only did they get riches for themselves, they also deprived the debt-ridden Spanish government of much needed money. In addition to the raiders from these enemy governments, the Spanish ships had to watch out for pirates, who were independent sea robbers eager to steal from anyone.

Sea warfare in those days was brutal. In the first stage of a battle, ships shot at each other with their big cannons. To fire its cannons, an attacking ship had to come up alongside its victim, since the cannons faced outward from the ship's sides. If the victim could not outrun or escape the attacker, its gun crews headed for the gun deck to fight back. They opened the gunports and

aimed the cannons. Some were pointed upward toward the attacking ship's masts and sails. Others were aimed at its hull and cannons.

A ship's cannons could be loaded with iron, stone, lead, or even brass balls. Lead balls sometimes were cast with bits of iron inside so that when they hit and split open, the iron pieces flew out and caused even more damage. Bar shot, usually shaped like a rod with balls at either end, could fly end over end through the air and tear apart the sails of an enemy's ship. Chain shot was similar, but it had a few links of chain in the middle. The cannons had to be loaded each time they were fired. As the cannon sent the shot forward, the gun itself lurched backward, or recoiled. Strong ropes kept it from rolling back too far.

Fire was a powerful weapon at sea, since ships were made of wood. To set an enemy's ship on fire, a ball with two big spikes was used. The spikes were covered with smaller spikes, and a tar-soaked rope was wrapped around them. The ball would burst into flame as it left the cannon and then, lodged in the hull of the enemy ship, would set it on fire.

When the first stage of the battle was over, the attacking ship moved closer to its

This beautiful bronze cannon is on exhibit at the entrance to the Archive of the Indies in Seville. Mel Fisher gave it to the people of Spain after recovering it from the Atocha.

During the days of the galleons, battles between fleets were brutal, as shown in this seventeenth-century painting by Pierre Puget.

victim, and its crew attempted to board. Then the defenders used smaller guns mounted on the upper decks. These guns could turn this way and that, firing balls, scrap iron, pebbles, and anything else that might damage the enemy. Other guns were also at hand. Muskets could blow off an attacker's arm or leg. A gun called a harquebus (HAR-kwih-bus) could do deadly damage.

If the attackers succeeded in boarding the ship, they were faced with sharp swords and daggers in addition to the guns. Although the men usually wore metal breast-plates and helmets, many lost their lives in these fierce fights.

The combatants often suffered horrible wounds. A ship's surgeon might have to cut off an arm or a leg to save a life. The patient's pain was terrible, as there were no anesthetics. There were no antibiotics, either, and wounds could become infected, killing the victim slowly.

5

THE *ATOCHA AS* TEACHER

The historic discovery of the lost Ghost Galleons has provided a treasure trove of information on Spain in its Golden Age. The items in the mother lode of the *Atocha* have been especially valuable, since they remained in place and were not scattered far and wide by storms.

The Mother Lode

The mother lode made an impressive sight lying on the bottom of the sea: a pile of ballast rocks and silver bars forty feet (12.2 meters) long, twenty feet (6.1 meters) wide, and five feet (1.5 meters) high. The

Archaeologist Duncan Mathewson examines a gold chain while others map the location of the sunken Atocha. ►

rocks and silver had protected the ship's wooden hull from the forces of nature for hundreds of years. As the wreck was uncovered, archaeologist Duncan Mathewson carefully measured and labeled the objects, noting just where each was found.

When the archaeologists compared the remains of the hull to the contract spelling out how the ship was to be constructed, they found that the builder had cheated. The contract called for three iron spikes and two wooden "treenails" to reinforce every place where the planks and the frame of the ship came together. But no treenails were found. Their absence weakened the hull's construction and probably aided in the breakup of the ship during the storms.

The wreck of the *Atocha* has helped us learn how people lived on board the galleons. Meals were prepared with iron skillets and copper pots. There was no galley, or ship's kitchen. Instead, cooking was probably done on deck, using bricks laid out on top of sand to form a hearth fueled by split wood. The remains of twenty-one kinds of animals were found, from turtles to deer. Most were used for food, although the rats and beetles were stowaways that ate the people's food. Some of the meat had been salted to preserve it for use later in the voyage, and some was fresh. Plant foods such as dried beans were also on board, both for people and for the live animals. Seeds of both grapes and pumpkins survived centuries underwater.

Interesting Objects

In addition to silver bars and coins, the *Atocha* carried many silver plates, candlesticks, cups, and other practical items. These have helped us understand more about life in seventeenth-century Spain and have also provided clues to some interesting objects.

Small silver pitchers, called ewers, are sometimes found in Spanish seventeenth-century paintings. Until some of these pitchers were found in the *Atocha*, people thought they were used for Catholic church ceremonies. In the paintings, they are marked *A* or *V*, which were believed to stand for *agua* (Spanish for "water") and *vino* ("wine"). But now we know that the pitchers were meant to hold oil

Two plain silver ewers marked A *and* V *are now known to be simple household containers for oil and vinegar.*

(*aceite*) and vinegar (*vinagre*). And they were used in ordinary households, just as glass salad-dressing cruets are used today.

A beautiful gilded silver cup from the *Atocha* may have helped solve another mystery. The cup is very similar to one in a painting made around 1620 by Spanish artist Juan Bautista de Espinosa. Large gilded platters are in the background of the painting. The cup stands in front of the platters and behind a group of four containers for salt and spices. Next to these is half an orange. Art historians long wondered what this painting was all about.

The cup from the *Atocha* may tell us. At the bottom of the cup—which doesn't show in the painting—is a rounded bump with a point.

Mining America's Treasure

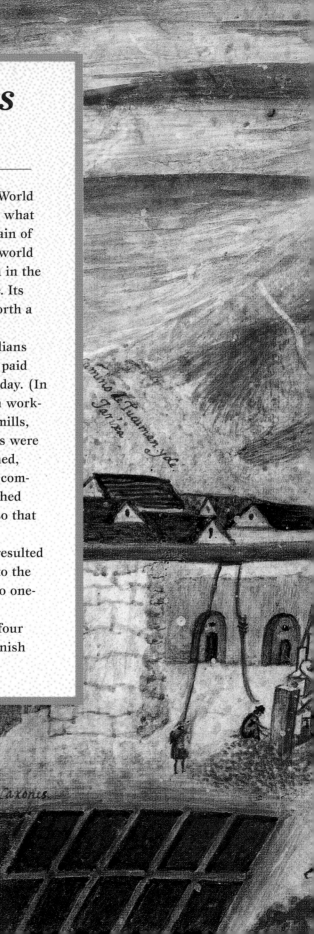

The greatest single source of wealth in the New World was the silver mine at Potosí (poh-toh-SEE), in what is now Bolivia. Potosí was an incredible mountain of silver for the taking, the biggest source of silver in the world in the 1600s. Potosí eventually became the largest town in the New World, developed to mine and refine the silver ore. Its name became legendary. In Spain today, the phrase "worth a Potosí" is used to describe a rich person.

Under Spanish colonial rule, every day 13,000 Indians worked as forced labor to dig the silver ore. They were paid only a tiny sum for their work: two and a half reales a day. (In Spain, twenty-four reales was a typical day's wage for a worker.) Other Indian laborers hauled the silver ore to the mills, where it was refined by still more native people. Llamas were used to carry the heavy loads of ore. The ore was crushed, then salt water and mercury were added. The mercury combined with the silver, so other substances could be washed away. Then, the silver-mercury mixture was squeezed so that the liquid mercury oozed out.

Mercury is a deadly poison, and working with it resulted in death for many Indians. The Potosí silver was vital to the Spanish king, for he received the *quinto*, his tax equal to one-fifth of the value of all the silver from the mountain.

The Potosí mine was highly productive for about four hundred years. In today's prices, the mine gave the Spanish empire more than $30 billion in silver.

This 1584 drawing shows the fabled silver mine at Potosí. Workers mine the silver ore from the mountain in the background. Pack llamas haul it to the refinery in the foreground.

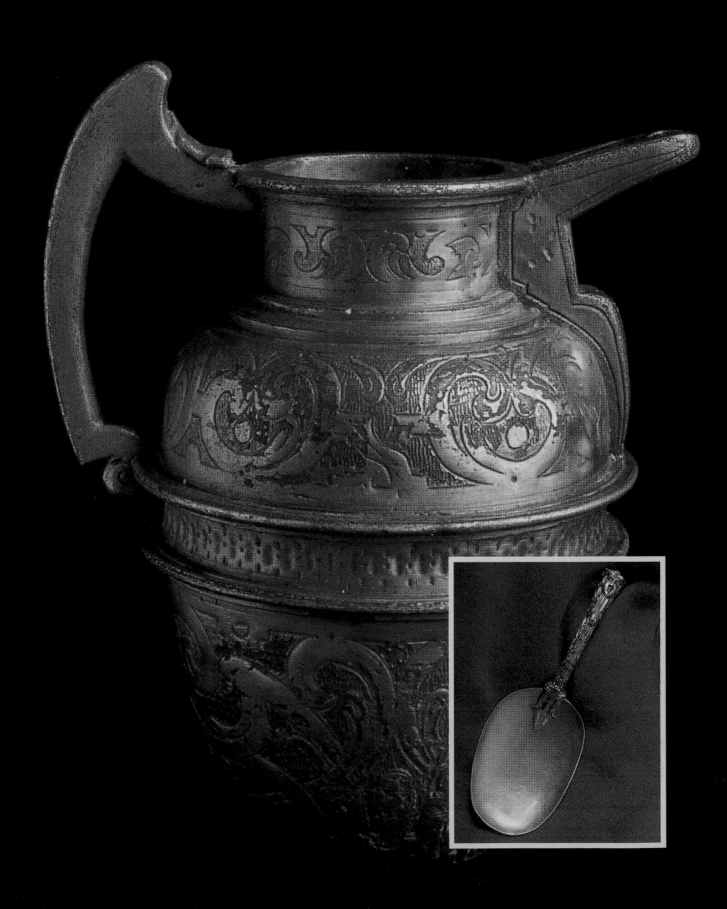

It may have been used to juice the orange. And the painting may have been about preparing a favorite drink, an alcoholic punch called a *hipocras*.

What the Designs Tell Us

Most of the silver items recovered from the Ghost Galleons are very simple in design, not fancy like the pieces that have survived in Spanish churches. They show that ordinary silver objects in Spain were similar to those used in England at the time. Historians had called the English designs "Puritan," because of their simplicity. But we now know that the same Puritan style was popular in strongly Catholic Spain. Perhaps both the Spanish and the English pieces in this simple style were made in the New World colonies and taken to Europe.

This elegant gilded silver cup was brought up from the Atocha *in 1985.*

◄ Opposite: *This gold pitcher was used in church services to hold water or wine. The gold spoon once had a wooden handle.*

Restoring the Artifacts

After lying under the sea for more than 375 years, the items from the wrecks were sometimes so completely encrusted by minerals and coral that they were difficult to recognize. Special techniques have been used to restore the artifacts.

The first step in restoring the clumps of coins is to soak them in a solution of a substance that turns the hard material around them into a mudlike goo. The goo is washed away, resulting in individual coins that are still slightly encrusted.

Next, the coins are treated using a chemical process called reverse electrolysis. Each coin is attached to a wire and suspended in a solution of the chemical sodium hydroxide. In the tank with the solution is a stainless steel plate. An electric current is passed through the coins. This causes the mineral deposits coating the coins to dissolve in the solution and move to the steel plate, freeing the coins themselves. The process takes about two days.

The coins are thoroughly rinsed, then polished by tumbling in a cylinder with small balls of steel for ten minutes. Then they are rinsed again. After this treatment, the best of the coins look as good as new.

The larger artifacts are kept in water until they are treated. First, they are X-rayed to see if the original metal is intact. If they're broken, they may be injected with rubber, which will take on the form of the artifact and hold any pieces together. A drill bit is used to carefully remove the layers of coral and other materials. Then the objects are treated with reverse electrolysis to remove rust and any remaining minerals. It can take weeks to remove the crust that has built up over more than 375 years.

Careful restoration can bring an encrusted silver pitcher, such as the one on the right, back to its original beauty, like the one on the left.

This delicate gold and red coral rosary is in perfect condition.

Some of the dishes brought up from the wreck tell us about the native peoples in the Americas. The Indians, for example, continued to use their familiar art and designs in their pottery, even when it was made for their conquerors. Some of the pieces show typical Indian designs, while others are a combination of Spanish and Indian styles.

Finding and interpreting the fascinating wreck of the *Atocha* has been and continues to be a team effort. Investors, adventurers, archaeologists, and historians are all involved. As time goes on, archaeologists will study the Ghost Galleons' artifacts and learn more and more about life in old Spain, in the New World, and on board a Spanish galleon. And since the hunt is still on for the missing parts of the *Atocha*, more exciting finds lie waiting to be discovered.

The Atocha in Time

Spain unified by
King Ferdinand and
Queen Isabella;
Columbus discovers
America
1492

Philip II
coronation
1556

 IN THE SPANISH WORLD

 IN EUROPE

1493
Leonardo da Vinci
draws a flying
machine

1540
Copernicus says
Earth revolves
around the Sun

Defeat of
Spanish
Armada
1588

Philip III
coronation
1598

Philip IV
coronation
1621

The
Atocha
sinks
1622

1591
Galileo develops
law of falling
bodies

1609
Galileo invents
telescope;
Kepler describes
laws of planetary
motion

1628
William Harvey
describes
complete
circulation of the
blood in the
human body

Glossary

anesthetic: A drug given to a person that keeps the body from feeling pain.

archaeologist: A scientist who studies tools, weapons, pottery, and other remains of human culture to find out how people used to live.

archive: A collection of records and documents of historical interest.

artifact: An item made by people in the past that has historical interest.

ballast: Material placed on a ship to add weight for stability. Large river rocks were used as ballast on galleons.

bow: The front end of a ship.

bowsprit: A mastlike pole that stuck forward from the bow of the galleon and carried two sails.

caravel: A small, light sailing ship used by the Spanish and Portuguese during the fifteenth and sixteenth centuries.

carrack: A large, heavy ship used from the fourteenth to sixteenth centuries, especially for carrying cargo.

ewer: A kind of pitcher.

forecastle: The covered area at the bow of a galleon.

galleon (GAL-ee-un): A well-armed ship designed to carry cargo on long ocean voyages.

galley: A large ship propelled by sails and oars, used for cargo and warfare in the Mediterranean Sea.

gilded: Covered with a thin layer of gold.

Gulf Stream: A current of warm water that flows northward along the southern coast of the United States and then turns eastward.

hull: The frame or body of a ship.

magnetometer: A device that measures the strength and direction of a magnetic field. It can detect metals at a distance.

mailbox: A special device, attached to the back of treasure-hunting boats, that directs a clear column of water down into the sea.

orlop: The deck below the gun deck on a galleon.

quinto (KEYN-toe)**:** A tax placed by the king of Spain on all precious metals brought from the New World to Spain; the *quinto* was equal to one-fifth of the value of the metals.

real (ray-AHL)**:** A coin containing one-eighth of an ounce of silver.

reef: A ridge of coral, rock, or sand that lies at or near the surface of the ocean or another body of water.

Renaissance: A period of great change in Western civilization that lasted from the fourteenth to the mid-seventeenth centuries.

salvage: To find and gather up the cargo from a shipwreck.

scuba: "Self-Contained Underwater Breathing Apparatus," an invention that allows a person to dive under the water freely, with the help of a face mask and oxygen tanks.

shot: Small round bits of metal fired from a gun. One blast shoots out a cluster of shot, which spreads out from the barrel.

Spanish Main: The seas controlled in the New World by Spain, from 1492 until the early 1800s.

stern: The rear end of a ship.

sterncastle: The built-up section at the rear of a galleon that provided housing for passengers and the captain.

treenail: A wooden peg made of compressed timber that would swell in its hole when it became wet.

For Further Reading

Gibbons, Gail. *Sunken Treasure*. New York: Harper Crest, 1988.

Lyon, Eugene. "*Santa Margarita*: Treasure from the Ghost Galleon." *National Geographic*, February 1982, pp. 228–243.

———. "The Trouble with Treasure." *National Geographic*, June 1976.

O'Byrne-Pelham, Fran. *The Search for the* Atocha *Treasure*. New York: Dillon Press, 1989.

Rutland, Jonathan. *See Inside a Galleon*. Edited by R. J. Unstead. New York: Warwick Press, 1986.

Sullivan, George. *Treasure Hunt: The Sixteen-Year Search for the Lost Treasure Ship* Atocha. New York: Henry Holt, 1987.

Websites *

http://www.atocha1622.com/ Some good historical information that expands on the book.

http://www.melfisher.com/ A fun site for all ages (music, too!)

*Websites change from time to time. For additional on-line information, check with the media specialist at your local library.

Bibliography

Budde-Jones, Kathryn. *Coins of the Lost Galleons*. Key West, FL: K. Budde-Jones, 1993.

Burkholder, Mark A., and Lyman L. Johnson. *Colonial Latin America*. New York: Oxford University Press, 1994.

Defourneaux, Marcelin. *Daily Life in Spain in the Golden Age*. Translated by Newton Branch. New York: Praeger Publishers, 1971.

Gold and Silver of the Atocha *and* Margarita (catalog). Auction June 14–15, 1988. New York: Christie's (auction house), 1988.

Harris, N. Neil. "Coins of the *Nuestra Señora de Atocha*." *The Numismatist*, October 1986, pp. 2,017–2,040.

Kirsch, Peter. *The Galleon: The Great Ships of the Armada Era*. Translated by Rachel Magowan. London: Conway Maritime Press, 1990.

Lyon, Eugene. *Search for the Mother Lode of the* Atocha. Port Salerno, FL: Florida Classics Library, 1989.

Mathewson, R. Duncan, III. *Treasure of the* Atocha. New York: E. P. Dutton, 1986.

Peterson, Mendel. *The Funnel of Gold*. New York: Little Brown and Co., 1975.

Rutland, Jonathan. *See Inside a Galleon*. Edited by R. J. Unstead. New York: Warwick Press, 1986.

Smith, Robert E. Kane, Robert C. Kammerling, Rhyna Moldes, Johy I. Koivula, and Shane F. McClure. "Emerald and Gold Treasures of the Spanish Galleon *Nuestra Señora de Atocha*." *Gems & Gemology*, winter 1989, 196–206.

Index

Page numbers for illustrations are in **boldface**

About the Author

Dorothy Patent is the author of more than one hundred science and nature books for children and has won numerous awards for her writing. She has a Ph.D. in zoology from the University of California, Berkeley.

Although trained as a biologist, Dorothy has always been fascinated by the human past. At home, next to the books about animals, her shelves are jammed with titles such as *Mysteries of the Past*. When the opportunity came to write about other times and cultures for children, Dorothy plunged enthusiastically into the project. In the process of researching the FROZEN IN TIME series, she said, "I have had some great adventures and have come to understand much more deeply what it means to be human."

Dorothy lives in Missoula, Montana, with her husband, Greg, and their two dogs, Elsa and Ninja. They enjoy living close to nature in their home at the edge of a forest.